Imperial

Murray McLeod

Copyright © Murray McLeod 2015

All rights reserved.

This book is copyright protected. Apart from any fair dealings for the purpose of private study, criticism, research or review as permitted under the *Copyright Act (Australia),* no part may be reproduced by any process without written permission from the copyright owner.

Photo reference: British Civil Aircraft (A.J. Jackson)

Picture History of Flight (Taylor)

Aviation/history

ISBN-13: 978-1506189567

ISBN-10: 1506189563

This book, and others by Murray McLeod may be purchased on www.amazon.com online bookstores and other retailers.

The author has taken all possible care to give appropriate acknowledgement and seek permissions from all interested parties and welcomes any further correspondence. Enquiries should be addressed to the copyright owner.

Author Profile

Australian author Murray McLeod is also an accredited artist/illustrator with several publications to his name. These are focussed on aviation history plus two motorcycle titles, 'TT Legends' and 'The Unapproachable Norton', covering road racing from the 1920's to the exciting post war period up to the 1960's. Another of his publications, and one that covers a vastly different arena is 'Aussie Tennis Legends', an appreciation of the esteem in which Australia was held over many decades of international and Davis Cup participation.

Email: mcleodart@westnet.com.au

http://www.mcleodart.com.au

Author Titles

Nonfiction

Aces and Adventurers

Aussie Tennis Greats

Flying Matilda

For Valour

Images of Eagles

The Unapproachable Norton

TT Legends

Fiction

Elliot's Odyssey

The Pilgrimage

*This book contains excerpts from two of Murray's other aviation books, *For Valour* and *Flying Matilda*.

Imperial Airways

The pioneering airline, which during the 1920's and 1930's created air routes through the most hostile of areas and generally under adverse conditions to place Great Britain as world leader in air travel during that period. Imperial's policy was to employ aircraft of British design wherever possible and in so doing advanced the cause of a great variety of British manufacturers.

With the closing down of Imperial in 1940 and the emergence of BOAC the employment of British-designed aircraft was to a large extent overshadowed by those of American origin. In a post-war situation this situation was continued, apart from several types being converted from wartime configuration.

The Avro Lancastrian, and Avro York fulfilled a valuable service for their time until purpose-built types emerged to make that transition to speedier and more comfortable world travel that has become available to generations of commuters the world over.

Dedication

To a band of of dedicated airmen in machines of marginal performance and safety who forged an array of international air routes.

Some made the supreme sacrifice in that pursuit, together with their hardy passengers in their efforts to create air services that overcame that tyranny of distance which bedevilled the intrepid traveller of previous decades.

Contents

Author Profile	3
Author Titles	4
Imperial Airways	5
Dedication	7
The Formative Years	11
Geoffrey de Havilland and Airco	16
DH34	18
Handley Page 0/400 and W8 series	21
Vickers Vimy and Vulcan	24
Vickers Vulcan	26
Armstrong Whitworth Argosy	29
European Argosies	30
DH66 Hercules	32
Supermarine Seaplanes	35
Short Flying Boats	40
Short S17 Kent Class	42
Avro 618 Ten Series	45
European Service	46
Boulton Paul and Avro	49
Boadicea and Britomart	50
Avro 652	52
Armstrong Whitworth Atalanta	55
The Australian experience	56
War Birds	57
De Havilland DH86	58
Into Service	58
Qantas Dramas	59
DH86 at War	61
Handley Page 42 and Short Scylla	63
Overseas and Home Operations	63

Short L17 Scylla	65
Scylla and Syrinx	66
Into Service	67
End of an Era	67
Short Empire Flying Boats S23 S30 S33	69
S30 and the Atlantic Air Mails	72
Short Mayo Composite	74
Atlantic Crossing	77
New York and Return	78
World's Record Attempt	78
Cape Town and Return	80
DH Albatross	81
Albatross on European Service	82
RAF Service	83
Armstrong Whitworth Ensign	85
Short 'G' Class boats	88
BOAC Ownership	89
Imperial Airways and British Airways Amalgamation	91
Flying Matilda	96
Pioneers of early Australian aviation	96
For Valour	104
Air VCs of World WAR II	104

The Formative Years

Following the 1918 Armistice and rapid demobilisation of the fledgling Royal Air Force, Great Britain was literally overflowing with war-surplus aircraft.

Iconic fighter types, like the Sopwith Camel and Dolphin clearly had no future in the civil domain; however less glamorous examples, typified by the successful DH4 day bomber and multi-engine 'heavies', such as the Handley Page 0/400 and Vickers Vimy offered distinct possibilities for civil operation.

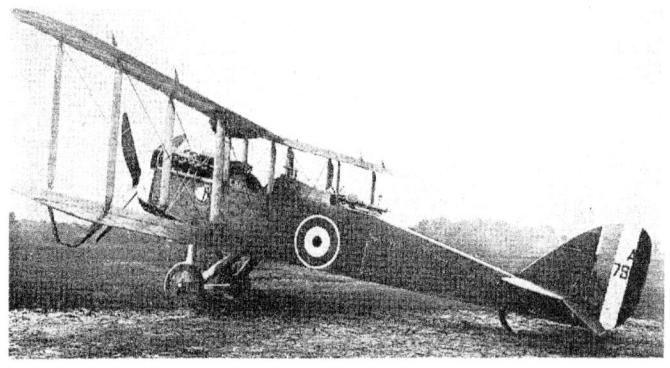

DH4

A number of private firms were formed in that early post-war period, and despite a lack of government subsidy they began passenger carrying services.

Air Transport and Travel Ltd was one of those pioneers and was active on the London-Paris route, initially using converted DH4s.

These were brand new examples and were modified for passenger service by the installation of an enclosed cabin behind the open pilot's cockpit. Two hardy passengers formed the total payload and by all accounts it was a noisy and uncomfortable experience; a situation not enhanced by the £20 fare; a considerable sum in those days.

Handley Page Air Transport was a major rival on the London-Paris route, and as the manufacturer of the 0/400 wartime bomber here was the obvious candidate for that service.

Eventually a number of 0/400s were converted for civil use; with 10 passengers installed on wicker chairs within the draughty fuselage; all this without sound-proofing and the benefit of windows to view the countryside.

Their experience was hardly an improvement on the DH4s used by Air Transport and Travel and a one-way ticket to Paris cost a hefty £25. It is still worth recording that the first British Certificate of Airworthiness fell to a HP 0/400; although the distinction of being G-EAAA, the first British civil registration was accorded to a converted DH9.

Handley Page 0/400

Daimler Hire Ltd. was another competitor in this fierce battle for airline supremacy; as were Instone Air Lines and British Marine Navigation.

Unlike continental airlines, which were enjoying government subsidies, those in the United Kingdom were not; so in the face of impossible competition these British firms were forced to review their operations. Now that air travel was no longer a novelty the government at last decided to offer a subsidy and follow the example of France, Belgium and Italy.

Short term subsidies were then granted to four operators for the following routes; Handley Page Air Transport Ltd (London-Paris), Daimler Airways Ltd. London-Manchester-Amsterdam), Instone Air Lines (London-Brussels-Cologne) and

British Marine Navigation (Southampton-Channel Isles).

The land operations were based at Croydon to the south of London; while the marine operations were conducted from venues such as Southampton and others along the south coast. A bureaucracy known as the Government Committee was eventually set up, and in 1924 the Hamblin Committee submitted its findings on the future of British airlines. As a result the decision was made to merge these four companies and bestow the title of Imperial Airways Ltd.

The amalgamation took place on 1st April 1924, and despite the inevitable problems in such a complex arrangement Imperial Airways at least gave stability to an emerging industry.

There was also financial relief for those dedicated travellers when the cost of a fare to Paris for example was reduced from a crippling £25 in 1922 to a realistic £5 by 1930. All that was in the future however; what now was needed were purpose-built airliners to replace the military types that soldiered on through those formative years. From the outset the emerging airline's focus was on forging international routes between Great Britain and European capitals and from its beginnings Imperial discontinued domestic service points 'north of Watford'.

Any aerial operations in that sector became charter flights. Imperial Airway's focus was the facilitation of overseas passenger travel to and from Britain's far-flung colonies. Up till then this was dependant on shipping, and as a result a series of survey flights were carried out between November 1925 and March 1926. At the forefront of these missions was renowned airman Alan Cobham and in that period he completed a comprehensive survey of the proposed London to Cape Town route, using a single-engine DH50 biplane.

In June 1926, just three months after the London-Cape Town venture, Cobham embarked on an even more ambitious survey flight, this time to Australia. Again he used the DH50, fitted with floats for the occasion. His route was via the Persian Gulf, through India and the Dutch East Indies, arriving at Port Darwin in August 1926.

Whilst at Darwin the DH50 was converted to landplane mode to carry out a tour of the Australian states, and on Cobham's return to Darwin the DH50 was re-fitted with floats for the return to England, arriving there on 1 October 1926, to complete a remarkable 28,000 miles survey flight.

Geoffrey de Havilland and Airco

Throughout that embryo period several manufacturers made substantial inputs in respect of the aircraft involved in early post war operations.

Handley Page and Vickers were a significant factor with their multi-engine types; while it was the creations of Geoffrey de Havilland that provided a quite fascinating mix of aircraft.

During World War 1 his designs were a major factor in that conflict, with these examples being built by the Aircraft Manufacturing Co. Ltd.; known universally as 'Airco'.

Perhaps his most significant creation was the 2-seat DH4 day bomber, which operated with British and American squadrons; while a number of brand new examples achieved civil status in the post war period.

DH4

Airco also produced 2000 DH 6 primary trainers during the conflict, and numbers of these also re-appeared in civil guise.

The DH9 day bomber was unpopular in squadron service but did find a niche with post war operators; while conversely the DH9a was an entirely different type of aircraft and soldiered on in RAF overseas service until 1930.

Various marques of the DH9a were popular with civil operators; however the first specifically designed airliner from Airco was the DH18. Powered by a 450hp Napier Lion it carried 8 passengers amidships in a large cabin, with the pilot located in an open cockpit to the rear of the upper wing.

The unnamed DH18 gave sterling service with various operators from 1920 to 1924, and the type could be regarded as the forerunner of a new generation of medium capacity airliners.

New designs were on the drawing board; still of biplane configuration but with the ability to achieve intercontinental status. Imperial Airways and other operators, notably KLM were beginning to reduce the tyranny of distance.

Such progress was enabled by a range of new designs, typified by the DH34, Armstrong Whitworth Argosy and DH Hercules.

DH 18

DH34

By 1921 the DH18 had been in service long enough for the economics of air transport to be understood. If commercial aviation were to pay its way, more payload would have to be carried per horsepower and at a higher speed.

De Havilland were quick to appreciate the situation, and using the DH18 as a foundation they proceeded through a series of variants; firstly with the 10-passenger monoplane DH29 and 8-seat biplane DH32 to create a more efficient design.

As yet the monoplane configuration had to find acceptance in the industry, and as a consequence de Havillands persisted with the basically-sound DH32 to create the now-famous DH34.

It retained the 450hp Napier Lion and featured seating for nine passengers in wicker chairs and an entry door large enough to permit carriage of a spare engine if necessary. Two pilots were carried in an open cockpit ahead of the upper wing rather than behind it, as on the DH18.

Daimler Hire operated DH34s on their London-Paris and London-Brussels routes, and between 1922 and 1924 they covered enormous mileages with both Daimler and Instone Airways.

Unfortunately the type was involved in several take-off and landing accidents; with two of them involving fatalities.

These were attributed to the high landing speed of 60mph, plus the absence of wheel brakes. Nevertheless the DH34 was a significant design in an emerging industry and continued in service until 1926.

DH34 luggage compartment plus in-flight steward

Handley Page 0/400 and W8 series

Following the 1918 armistice Handley Page Air Transport Ltd. was an early participant in post war British air travel. Their 0/400 heavy bomber saw limited wartime service; however in civil guise it fulfilled a useful role in passenger and freight transport.

Accommodation for the eight passengers was far from luxurious but until the end of 1920 the type could claim a fine safety record as they plied their continental routes. Unfortunately, in that December G-EAMA was lost in a disastrous take-off crash.

HP 0/400

However the 0/400 could only be regarded as an interim type and by 1922 an up-dated version, the

W8 was coming into service. It was lighter and aerodynamically cleaner; with two pilots in an open cockpit forward of a roomy, well-glazed cabin for 15 passengers.

For its time the W8 far excelled its contemporaries in performance; with the type being improved in later marques, such as the W9 and W10. Outwardly the most obvious change in the W8 was a single fin and rudder, compared to the box-like twin rudder arrangement of the bomber.

In June 1921 the Air Ministry announced a three year plan for assisting the airlines and was empowered by Treasury to authorise construction of a limited number of aircraft for lease to approved firms. As a result three modified W8b aircraft were ordered; with these 12-seater versions maintaining the London-Paris-Brussels services of the company until they were absorbed into Imperial Airways in April 1924.

In an attempt to reduce the possibility of accidents through engine failure the W8e was developed with one Rolls Royce Eagle in the nose to supplement the outboard Siddeley Pumas.

One example of this version, known as the 'Hamilton' was introduced, and this led to a more powerful version, the W9 'Hampstead', which carried 14 passengers in the traditional wicker chairs in a heated cabin. These tri-motor variants were introduced into Imperial service during 1925, and for several years they delivered reliable and safe travel. This situation could not be applied to the earlier W8s, which were involved in three fatal accidents over the ensuing years of their service.

By 1931 the aged W series were retired from airline operation; with some being used as joy-riders in Aviation Day displays that were popular in the early 1930s.

HP W8

Vickers Vimy and Vulcan

Like its contemporary the Handley Page 0/400 the Vimy saw only limited war service in their proposed role as heavy bombers.

However in the post-war RAF it was used extensively, in particular in the Middle East during the 1920s. The type also featured in two spectacular civil flights in 1919; first of these was the historic Atlantic crossing of June14/15.

Piloted by John Alcock and navigated by Arthur Whitten Brown the Vimy took off from St. John's Newfoundland and after an incident-filled passage they touched down in a heavy landing at Clifden Ireland, sixteen hours later; thus completing the first non-stop Atlantic crossing.

In November of that year an Australian crew made the first England-Australia flight as part of a contest to complete the journey in less than 30 days. Brothers Ross and Keith Smith were pilot and co-pilot, with mechanics Bennett and Shiers completing the crew.

Considering the distances involved and limited facilities en-route this was a remarkable achievement for the intrepid fliers to complete the journey in 27days and 20 minutes.

Vickers Vimy (England/Australia flight)

British air transport pioneer Instone also took delivery of Vimy Commercial (G-EASU) for its inaugural Croydon-Brussels service. In October 1922 the Vimy became the first civil aircraft to make a scheduled flight to Cologne, via Brussels in a time of 3hrs 25 minutes.

Still powered by two Rolls Royce Eagles these commercial versions featured a rounded fuselage design with two pilots and accommodation for 10 passengers.

Compared to the larger Handley Page airliners the Vimy was built in relatively small numbers and is better remembered for its RAF service; with ongoing variants such as the Vernon,

Victoria and Valentia, which served as transports, troop carriers and ambulance aircraft, mainly in the Middle East areas.

Vimy Commercial

Vickers Vulcan

The single-engine Vulcan first flew in May 1922; being an attempt to build a commercial aircraft that would hopefully be able to pay its way without government subsidy. Its appearance was that of great rotundity, with accommodation for 8 passengers, a pilot and baggage.

During early trial flights the Vulcan displayed a reluctance to perform at its designated maximum weight, despite being powered by the trusted Rolls Royce Eagle.

Nevertheless, Vickers proceeded with the construction of eight more Vulcans. Instone Air

Lines acquired three examples, which were chiefly employed on their London-Brussels service. With their obese appearance and snub noses these remarkably ugly aircraft were bestowed the permanent title of 'Flying Pigs'.

In 1922 two Vulcans were shipped to Australia for evaluation by the emerging Qantas organisation. However, they proved quite unable to handle the harsh summer environment of Central Queensland and were shipped back to England.

The Vulcan's lack of power reserve was further underlined by the loss of Instone's G-EBDN in a crash in Surrey in 1923.

This situation led to the installation of the more powerful Napier Lion in the last two Vulcans built; with both aircraft entering Imperial service in December 1924.

A third Vulcan (G-EBLB) was acquired in the following May, but their Imperial tenure was relatively brief and in 1926 they were relegated to charter work. After amassing a considerable air mileage the final Vulcan (G-EBLB) was destroyed in a fatal crash at Purley in July 1928.

Vickers Vulcan

Armstrong Whitworth Argosy

At its formation in 1924 Imperial Airways took over from its predecessors 13 aircraft of four different types; more than half of which were single-engine DH34s.

Realizing that its own survival depended on the creation of a reputation of safety, Imperial decided that all future designs must be multi-engine.

As a result, orders were placed with De Havilland, Handley Page, and Armstrong Whitworth, who in 1926 delivered a combined total of 12 two and three-engine airliners into Imperial service.

For Armstrong Whitworth this was their first venture into multi-engine aircraft. During World War 1 the firm produced a range of 2-seat army co-operation biplanes, known as the FK series.

They performed a vital but unglamorous role in that conflict, and post-war their Siskin fighter equipped eleven RAF squadrons.

FK8

Their new airliner emerged as the Argosy, a large three-engine biplane with seating for 20 passengers in a long, square section fuselage. In the style of the period, two pilots were seated side by side in an open cockpit in the nose. The new Argosy was strictly utilitarian in appearance, but with its steel tube construction it proved to be a most durable airliner. Power was provided by three 385hp Siddeley Jaguar radials, which gave a cruising speed of 90mph and range of 400 miles.

European Argosies

Three Argosy 1s were delivered during 1926 and 1927 and put into regular service to Paris, Basle, Brussels and Cologne. Each aircraft was named after a principal United Kingdom city and later versions carried a buffet and steward in place of the two rear seats. In 1929 three additional Argosies entered services on the European routes, and later these were extended to Salonika on the newly-introduced England-India service. These Argosy IIs were 28-seaters, fitted with more powerful 420hp Siddeley Jaguar radials.

In 1929 the fleet was joined by a seventh and last Argosy; and in the style of efficient airliners they gave sterling and uneventful service until 1931 when G-AACH was destroyed by fire following a crash by a pilot qualifying for multi-engine endorsement. Argosies continued in service until 1935, with their hitherto unblemished passenger record sadly marred by the mysterious loss of 'City of Liverpool' in a mid-air fire over Belgium in March 1933.

This unfortunate episode could well be regarded as an early example of aerial sabotage. The Argosy was finally retired in 1934 after ten years of meritorious service; with the final example ending its days in 1936 providing joy-rides around Blackpool Tower.

Argosy II 'City of Birmingham'

DH66 Hercules

In 1925 Britain's De Havilland's was entrusted with the design of an airliner capable of operating in the inhospitable desert areas of the Middle East.

This was the result of an agreement with the Air Ministry, whereby Imperial Airways would open a regular fortnightly passenger, freight and airmail service between Cairo and Karachi. Such an arrangement would relieve the responsibility of the RAF running the existing desert air mail, while Imperial were to receive a government subsidy of £500,000 annually for five years.

The DH 66 emerged as a large two-bay biplane with a cruising speed of 110 mph and accommodation for 7 passengers, luggage and mail.

To minimise the risk of forced landings, the Hercules as it was named was powered by three Bristol Jupiter air-cooled radials of 420hp. After acceptance trials and crew training the desert route was inaugurated in December 1926.

Five aircraft of the original contract were delivered by March 1927, after which the fleet settled down to earn a reputation for utter reliability.

'City of Cairo'

Western Australian Airways also ordered four Hercules for their Perth/Adelaide service. They were similar to the original Imperial order except for an enclosed pilot's cabin and a tail wheel to replace the primitive tail skid. Their Hercules fleet represented a huge advance over its predecessors when it began operating in 1929. In Australian service the passenger accommodation was doubled to fourteen, with luxury innovations for the time that included leather-upholstered chairs and a toilet compartment.

Imperial also ordered further Hercules, to the same format as Western Australian Airlines; one of these, 'City of Jerusalem' (G-EBMZ) unfortunately crashed in a night landing and was destroyed by fire. 'City of Johdpur' (G-ABCP) became its replacement, following its purchase from Western Australian Airlines.

In April 1931 Imperial carried out two experimental airmail deliveries to Australia, but the first of these ran short of fuel in appalling weather and was wrecked in a forced landing 10 miles from Koepang in Java.

The mail was quickly retrieved by Kingsford Smith in the Fokker tri-motor 'Southern Cross' and flown to Darwin. Once more Western Australian Airways provided the replacement; this one becoming Imperial's final Hercules, 'City of Cape Town' (G-ABMT)

The stately Hercules was one of the last examples of a large biplane airliner and was remembered as a significant design from those pioneering years.

Western Australian Hercules VH-UJP

Supermarine Seaplanes

For centuries Great Britain was a sea-faring nation; so in an emerging aviation industry a progression to sea-going aircraft would seem to a logical development.

A firm with an ongoing involvement in float planes was the Southampton-based Supermarine Aviation Works. They were also fortunate in having Reginald J. Mitchell as their chief designer, who in later years gained enduring fame as the creator of the immortal Spitfire.

However in the early post war period his focus was directed firmly to marine aircraft; with a particular interest in the Schneider Trophy contest. While outside the scope of Imperial Airways history these classic racers still merit an inclusion.

This prestigious event was inaugurated in 1913 as a contest between nations; primarily as reliability contest and was restricted to float planes.

Great Britain emerged as winners of the 1914 event with the diminutive Sopwith Schneider; and in the 1922 race held at Naples the Supermarine Sea Lion II achieved another victory for Britain.

For the 1925 Trophy held in Baltimore victory went to The United States with their Curtiss R3C biplane, however at the 1927 event held at Venice, Great Britain claimed first and second places with Mitchell's S5 monoplane.

During the race Flt.Lt. Webster raised the World Speed Record over 100 kms. to 283.66 mph.

Supermarine S5

Two S6 seaplanes were built for the 1929 Schneider Race held over the Solent, and again Britain was successful; the winning S6 averaging 328.63 mph. Shortly afterwards Sqrn. Ldr. Orlebar raised the World Speed Record to 357.7 mph.

1931 found Britain in the trough of a financial crisis and a British entry for the Schneider Contest was only assured at the last moment through the generosity of the late Lady Houston.

Two of the 1929 S6 machines were therefore modified, the principal change being new floats, carrying more petrol and the installation of greater water-cooling areas. The modified type was known as S6A.

Two new machines, designated S6B were constructed in little more than six months. In order to provide adequate cooling for the Rolls Royce racing engine, which developed 2,330 hp. at full throttle, almost the whole of the wing surfaces and upper part of the floats formed water-cooling radiators.

On 13 September 1931, the S6B; flown by Flt. Lt. J.N. Boothman won the Schneider Trophy outright for Great Britain, averaging 340.08 mph. over the Solent course, and on 29 September, Flt. Lt. G. Stainforth, flying an S6B boosted to 2,600 hp. set up a new World Speed Record of 407.5 mph.

Supermarine S6B

Apart from Mitchell's Schneider Trophy involvement, the firm was also involved in the manufacture of civil aircraft; one example was the Sea Eagle cabin amphibian; a biplane with seating for six passengers. Its 350hp Rolls Royce Eagle was installed behind the wings, operating as a pusher unit.

Two aircraft, G-EBGR and G-EBGS were handed over to Imperial Airways in June 1924. After five years of operation by the British Marine Air Navigation Co. around the Channel Islands, 'GR was withdrawn from service, while 'GS had the misfortune to be sunk in a collision with a ship in January 1927.

The hull was later salvaged, stored at Hythe, and finally burned at Heston in 1953.

Supermarine Sea Eagle G-EGBS

Aside from the small Channel boats operated by Imperial, Supermarine was a major supplier of large biplane flying boats for RAF service and 'showing the flag' in many parts of the world.

These long-distance formation flights had their origins with No.480 Coastal Reconnaissance squadron.

In October 1927 four Southamptons made a memorable cruise from Felixstowe, flying to Singapore via the Mediterranean and India, afterwards visiting Australia and Hong Kong, returning to Singapore in December 1928 to complete a memorable cruise in open-cockpit machines.

Short Flying Boats

The S8 Calcutta, designed to a 1927 specification for Imperial Airways was the first British flying boat with an all-metal hull; in this instance corrosion-resisting duralumin.

It was a large biplane powered by three Bristol Jupiter radials for multi-engine safety, with comfortable accommodation for 15 passengers and a steward, and two pilots in the traditional open cockpit. In RAF service they type was named the Rangoon.

These stately craft were designed to operate on the Mediterranean section of the Imperial route to India. In April 1929; following successful test flights and crew training the first Calcutta (G-EBVG) left for Genoa to inaugurate the service.

Passengers of that era would have needed a degree of stamina to undertake a flight to India. First stage was by Armstrong Whitworth Argosy to Basle, thence by sleeping car express to Genoa and continuing by Short Calcutta to Alexandria via 6 intermediate stops.

The final stage to Karachi was flown by DH Hercules; the whole service operating to a seven day schedule.

A third Calcutta (G-AADN) was commissioned in March 1929, but in October it was destined to founder with all hands including Capt. Birt the pilot during a storm off Spezia. These could be demanding situations for the pioneering Calcutta pilots; with a limited range of 650 miles and 75 knots cruising speed this left nothing in hand when strong headwinds were encountered.

It was often a case of abandoning a flight before the point of no return was reached and the pilot make his way back to their previous departure point; fortunately relief was in hand with a more powerful version soon to enter service.

Short S8 Calcutta 'City of Athens'

Short S17 Kent Class

The replacement was the 'Kent' class boat; and apart from the additional engine and noticeable increase in size, the design closely followed the general lines of the Calcutta.

Sixteen passengers were carried in Pullman-style luxury, while the pilots also enjoyed a degree of comfort in an enclosed cabin.

Three boats were initially ordered by Imperial Airways; with the prototype 'Scipio' (G-ABFA) making a trouble-free test flight in February 1931.

After routine trials 'Scipio' was ferried to the Mediterranean on 5 May 1931, followed ten days afterwards by 'FB 'Sylvanus'. A third boat 'FC 'Satyrus' joined the fleet some time later. By August 1932 the three Kents had flown an impressive number of miles on the Brindisi-Alexandria run without a single mechanical breakdown.

Meantime the original Calcuttas operated the difficult Khartoum-Kisumu section of the route to South Africa, opened in January 1932. Over the ensuing three years the combined fleet of seven boats gave uninterrupted service; until a series of misfortunes befell them.

This was a period when fascist Italy was at war with a defenceless Abyssinia. In that country's defence the rather pathetic League of Nations responded by imposing meaningless sanctions on Italy, which were totally ignored. Imperial Airways used Brindisi as an overnight stop-over, and in retaliation the passengers were subjected to anti-British demonstrations outside their hotel.

These threats were more theatrical than real and bore little comparison to the behaviour of their bullying cohorts, the Nazis. Nevertheless, 'Sylvanus' was set on fire and destroyed at its moorings at Brindisi in November 1935.

Even more saddening was the loss of Calcutta G-AASJ, 'City of Khartoum', which foundered in a sudden forced landing outside Alexandria Harbour in December, with the death of 12 passengers.

To compound their setbacks, eight months later the veteran 'Scipio' crashed on alighting at Mirabella in Crete in exceptionally bad weather; again with tragic loss of life.

It was the closing chapter for the Mediterranean fleet and finally in September 1935, after more than seven years of service two of the surviving Calcuttas were ferried back to England.

Based at Southampton they were re-engined and spent their remaining years as crew trainers for the new S23 Empire boats that would introduce new standards of excellence in air travel.

Short S17 'Satyrus'

Avro 618 Ten Series

As the decade of the 'Roaring Twenties' drew to a close it was clear that air travel had survived its adolescent years and was here to stay.

What the industry needed at this point were fresh designs to supplant the ageing biplane types that had forged those early routes.

During the mid-1920s the FVII Fokker series entered service on both sides of the Atlantic; and such was its popularity, in particular the FVIIB tri-motor that in 1928 Avro acquired a licence to build an Anglicised version.

In British service it was known as the Avro Ten; so named simply because it carried eight passengers and two crew members.

It differed only slightly in detail to its Dutch prototype, and was powered by three 215 hp Siddeley Lynx rather than the usual Wright Whirlwinds.

European Service

The Avro Ten was built in only small numbers, with the type entering Imperial service in early 1930. Their function was general charter work, mainly on European routes, operating out of Croydon and also Le Bourget.

In British service the Avro Ten underwent various modifications that culminated in the graceful twin-engine Avro 18; however these versions were not used by Imperial Airways. In reality the Avro Ten gained more fame in Australian service; however in 1931 this all changed to notoriety.

Five Avro Tens were supplied to Charles Kingsford Smith for operation on his newly established Australian National Airways.

Its flagship 'Southern Cloud' made headline news in March 1931 when it disappeared without trace while on a scheduled Sydney-Melbourne passenger flight. Gale force winds and torrential rain were predicted for the plane's route, and in the extreme conditions the pilot, Captain Shortridge may have presumed to be well clear of the mountains and began a let-down to what he believed to be the outskirts of Melbourne; instead he crashed to destruction in the loneliest of areas.

The 'Southern Cloud' mystery remained unsolved for decades until the wreck was located in October 1958, when a bush walker stumbled onto its skeletal remains in a remote area of the Snowy Mountains.

Scientific examination revealed that it had flown into a hillside under full power in stormy conditions with no survivors. Southern Cloud's discovery was a somewhat grim affair but at least an enduring mystery in Australian air travel had at last been resolved

The initial loss of 'Southern Cloud', with the resulting adverse publicity and search costs was a virtual death blow for Australian National Airways which shortly afterwards closed down its operations.

Unlike its main competitor Qantas, which enjoyed generous government subsidies ANA was completely independently operated, without the buttress of government aid. Only for the loss of

'Southern Cloud', it would be reasonable to assume that Australian airline operation would be vastly different to the situation that exists in the current era.

Boulton Paul and Avro

During the late 1920s Boulton and Paul Ltd were manufacturers best known for a succession of military biplanes. Their P26 Sidestrand of 1926 operated with just one RAF squadron; No101, and during their tenure they demonstrated aerobatic prowess not normally associated with twin-engine biplanes.

These were replaced by an improved variant, the Overstrand, still similar in layout and fitted with a hydraulic gun turret; enabling gunners to improve their accuracy by significant margins in air-to-air combat drill.

Boulton Paul Overstrand

Aside from their military input the firm was involved in the construction of two types of civil transports; one for mail, the other for passengers.

First of these was the P64 Mailplane; a rather compact biplane of all-metal construction. Powered by two 550hp Bristol Pegasus engines G-ABYK first flew in March 1933; fulfilling its design specifications in every way.

An unfortunate setback was later experienced when the aircraft collided with a fence. Repairs were soon effected and after modifications it was back in service.

However its career was destined to be short-lived when in October 1933 the Mailplane was completely destroyed in a crash.

Boulton Paul Mailplane

Boadicea and Britomart

Its replacement was the P71A, powered by two 490hp Siddeley Jaguar engines, that lessened its performance to some degree, but with its lengthened fuselage and triple fin arrangement it emerged as a more handsome machine.

For Imperial Airways operation it was initially arranged to carry 14 passengers, but instead it was fitted out in luxury 7 seat format.

The two aircraft; G-ACOX 'Boadicea' and G-ACOY 'Britomart' were delivered to Croydon in February 1935; mainly for use on VIP and special charter flights. But like their progenitor the P64 their careers were fated to be cut short when both were destroyed in crashes.

'Britomart' was the first to be lost, when it was damaged beyond economical repair following a heavy landing at Brussels on 25 October 1935.

Fortunately all seven passengers and two crew members escaped with minor injuries. 'Boadicea's' fate however was more sinister; following its departure from Croydon on 25 September 1936, carrying Continental mail. After the wireless operator reported its position over the English coastline nothing more was ever heard of it.

A month later the body of the pilot was washed ashore on the French coast, together with some wreckage. 'Boadicea' had clearly crashed into the sea but the cause was never deduced.

Boulton Paul P71A 'Britomart'

Avro 652

As the 1930s progressed, airliner fashion was clearly focussed on the twin-engine low wing monoplane with retractable undercarriage. Such a trend was indelibly demonstrated with the introduction of the DC2 and its competitor the Boeing 247

Avro followed this trend rather neatly by adapting their Fokker-style airframe, as employed on the Avro Ten series to the new configuration by simply locating the wing underneath.

The result was the Avro 652; two examples of which were built and delivered to Imperial Airways; entering service in March 1935. Powered by two 290hp Cheetah VI engines they were named 'Avalon' (G-ACRM) and 'Avatar' (G-ACRN).

For a number of years they operated in unwavering fashion on the Croydon-Brindisi route, carrying four passengers and crew of two. With the onset of

World War II the pair was sold to Air Service Training Ltd. as navigational trainers.

Despite their serving in only limited numbers the contribution of this duo to Imperial Airways could not be regarded as insignificant.

Avro 652 'Avalon' G-ACRM

A military counterpart, the well-remembered Avro 652A Anson made its first flight in March 1935 and was the forerunner of some 11,000 built over the next 17 years.

Initially they operated with Coastal Command in the reconnaissance role, until supplanted by more efficient types, such as the Lockheed Hudson and Short Sunderland. Ansons continued to serve in a multitude of roles in RAF service, including crew trainers, communications and many others.

Avro 652a Anson

In a post-war situation the series 2 Anson, featuring a new tapered wing, more internal headroom and hydraulically operated undercarriage gave valuable service with operators in the United Kingdom, Canada and Australia.

Armstrong Whitworth Atalanta

The Armstrong Whitworth AW15 Atalanta was the firm's second type to enter Imperial service, whose requirement was for a machine to operate solely on the overseas sections of their trunk routes to South Africa and Australia.

The AW 15 emerged as a high wing monoplane of exceptionally clean design; powered by four 340hp Siddeley engines.

In an age of biplanes its streamlined profile bore little comparison to its erstwhile predecessor, the angular Argosy tri-motor.

Nine passengers were carried in a saloon of generous dimensions to alleviate the discomforts of tropical flying; with the payload of mail and freight being equally divided between passengers and cargo.

The prototype G-ABPI made its appearance in June 1932, carrying the name 'Atalanta'; and for a time it was involved in tests and crew training.

This programme received a setback when 'Atalanta' suffered considerable damage in a forced landing; and to minimise adverse publicity for a new and untried type; after repairs the prototype was renamed 'Arethusa'.

The name 'Atalanta' was then switched to the fourth production aircraft, G-ABTI, and on 1 January 1933 it left Croydon on the first proving flight to the Cape. Some delays with engine trouble were experienced at Cairo; with Cape Town being reached on 14 February.

Shortly afterwards the Atalantas began regular services, replacing the DH Hercules on that route; with an overall time of eleven days; nowadays a Boeing 747 would cover the distance in 11 hours.

The Australian experience

A similar proving flight to Australia was organized; and on 29 May 'Astrea' was despatched with the intention of connecting with a Qantas DH86 at Singapore.

As it happened 'Astrea' was taken straight through to Australia, reaching Darwin safely despite an emergency landing on Bathurst Island to the north.

The 14000 mile overall flight to Melbourne was completed on 30 June; after which the machine was ferried back to its operational base at Karachi.

'Astrea's' pilot was Captain A.R. Prendergast, (later to lose his life in the crash of Qantas DH86 VH-USG south-east of Longreach on 15 November 1934).

During 1933 the Eastern route was extended from Karachi to Calcutta; plus a service to Singapore. At that time a subsidiary company, Indian Transcontinental Airways Ltd. was formed to manage this section of the route, which saw the Atalantas spending their careers in Indian markings.

War Birds

For eight years they continued to operate their tropical schedules in an unobtrusive manner, and with the outbreak of war in the Pacific the Atalantas were impressed for service with the Indian Air Force.

They finished their useful days on coastal anti-submarine patrols; with several being lost in accidents until the type was finally retired in June 1944.

A.W.15 'Atalanta' G-ABPI

De Havilland DH86

The unnamed DH86 was designed in 1933 to meet a Qantas specification for use on the Singapore-Australia section of the proposed Imperial air route.

With multi-engine security considered to be a priority the DH 86 was powered by four 200hp Gypsy engines. However in an era of new all-metal monoplanes it was still a biplane; albeit well proportioned and of graceful design.

Also, in the De Havilland manner; it was constructed of timber framework with fabric covered plywood panels, which imparted an air of fragility to a prospective airliner intended to carry 10 passengers.

Into Service

After exhaustive flight testing, the prototype 'Diana' entered service on 24 May 1934 on mail services within the British Isles.

The original production batch featured a single-pilot arrangement, which was unacceptable to Qantas who insisted on a two-pilot variant; this version known as the DH86A.

All future models appeared in this format, including the prototype 'Diana', which was thus modified and re-appeared as 'Delphinus' in full Imperial livery.

Six similar aircraft, destined for Qantas operation were then despatched to Australia; two by air and four as deck cargo. Unfortunately VH-USG was totally destroyed at Longreach in central Queensland while on the final stage of its delivery flight; all crew members being killed.

Crash scene investigators expressed concern at apparent defects in the forward fin post; posing the question that a failure in that component caused its loss.

Qantas Dramas

A further dilemma was the widely advertised Brisbane-Singapore air mail; scheduled to commence on 10 December 1934. With the airworthiness of the DH86 in question Qantas reverted to two of their elderly DH61s to inaugurate the service. Qantas were sufficiently concerned to question De Havilland's workmanship, and at one stage they contemplated making legal claims against them.

Meanwhile a second DH86 (VH-USD) was found to have the fin bias mechanism cracked in the manner of VH-USG. Qantas carried out its own modification and with Civil Aviation Branch approval the DH86 entered Qantas service. As a precaution, for a three month period no fare-paying passengers and only mail was carried.

Qantas VH-USC

Qantas was not the only Australian operator to experience DH86 losses. Holyman's Airways took delivery of three examples during 1934-35 for use on their Melbourne-Launceston route.

On 19 October 1934 'Miss Hobart', with a full complement of passengers vanished virtually without trace over Bass Strait.

Twelve months later 'Loina' (VH-URT) suffered a similar fate; although some wreckage was retrieved, not enough however to pinpoint the cause of the disaster.

It is worth noting that on 20 February 1942 VH-USE crashed to destruction shortly after leaving Brisbane's Archerfield airport.

Crash investigators arrived on the scene, only to find that the wreckage had been deliberately burnt; thus denying any opportunity to solve the airworthiness enigma.

Significantly the aircraft's fin was discovered intact almost a mile from the crash site, showing clearly that it had detached itself in the air. Perhaps that troublesome unit was determined to have the last word in a chain of tragedies.

Tragic as it was the loss of VH-USE received scant publicity due to the destructive Japanese air raids on Darwin that very day, when the Australian continent first came under attack.

DH86 at War

A total of 62 DH86s was built, 44 of them being of British registry. During 1935-36 Imperial Airways took delivery of 12 examples, which entered service on their European, West African and Far East schedules.

They were also widely used by other British operators in the period up to World War II. At the commencement of hostilities some were impressed for ferrying supplies to France, where regrettably 'Neptune' and 'Venus' were lost in action.

Other examples performed useful roles as navigator and wireless operator trainers in RAF and RAAF service, and also as air ambulances in the Western Desert.

Handley Page 42 and Short Scylla

These stately machines were the largest biplanes operated by Imperial Airways. Powered by four 550hp Bristol Jupiter radials the Hannibal and Heracles class came into service in 1931.

Their unsophisticated appearance at first drew ribald criticism but they rapidly established a reputation for reliability and comfort. Designed for economical cruising at around 100mph they set up new standards of safety in air travel.

Total production consisted of four aircraft of each of two versions; four of those based at Cairo for services to Cape Town and Karachi were known as the HP42E or Eastern model; with accommodation for 24 passengers.

Four HP42W or Western models operated out of Croydon to service European routes; these versions carried 38 passengers.

Overseas and Home Operations

Each of these grand aircraft was accorded a heroic title; with 'Hannibal' inaugurating the London-Paris service in June 1931.

In August however, 'Hannibal' was involved in a forced landing near Tunbridge; and after repairs it was transferred to Cairo to join 'Hadrian' and 'Hanno' on the Eastern routes.

In Western operations the HP42s gave long and meritorious service; a classic example was 'Heracles', which after seven years of operation had flown 1½ million miles and carried 95,000 passengers.

Figures for their Eastern counterparts were equally impressive; with 'Helena' carrying the first through air mail to Cape Town in January 1932.

'Hengist' performed a similar function in December 1934; on this occasion with the first through air mail to Australia.

Unfortunately, soon afterwards 'Hengist' was destroyed in a hangar fire at Karachi; and in that year 'Hanno' returned home and was converted to HP42W configuration to replace 'Hengist' on European routes.

They all continued in service until September 1939, despite the introduction of a new breed of monoplane airliners; but the war years were particularly unkind to these pioneering veterans.

In November 1939 'Horatius' was destroyed in a forced landing at Devon.

Meantime, the three surviving HP42E models were flown home; but regrettably the veteran 'Hannibal' was lost in the Indian Ocean in March1940. 'Hanno' and 'Hercules' were not spared either, when both were destroyed in a gale at Whitchurch, also in March 1940.

The last survivor 'Helena' was eventually dismantled, with its metal fuselage mounted on trestles and used as a squadron office at a Royal Navy shore establishment.

Handley Page 42E 'Hannibal' G-AAGX

Short L17 Scylla

The introduction of the HP42 into Imperial Airways service partly filled the need for a larger airliner.

Originally four were allocated to the European area, but two were transferred to Empire routes, leaving only 'Heracles' and 'Horatius' on European service. They could be supplemented by the ageing Argosies, but one of these, 'City of Liverpool' was lost early in 1933.

Scylla and Syrinx

Handley Page proposed a modified version of the HP42, the HP45 but with a price tag of £42,000 (almost double that of the original) Imperial rejected the offer.

They then approached Short Brothers with the proposal that they build two large landplanes based on the S17 Kent class flying boat, employing identical wings, tail unit and engines in order to save both time and money.

Being seaplane specialists it was something of a novelty for Shorts to become involved in landplanes. The two aircraft, named 'Scylla' and 'Syrinx' were built side-by-side in the seaplane works at Rochester beside the River Medway, and by January 1934 'Scylla' had been assembled.

However the seaplane works had no aerodrome, which entailed dismantling the aircraft and transporting the components to Rochester aerodrome for final assembly. Due to the sheer size of the aircraft it could only be assembled in the open; a laborious and uncomfortable procedure in mid-winter. In spite of these problems 'Scylla' was ready for test flights on March 26.

Into Service

These proved satisfactory, and following a period of crew training 'Scylla' made its first service flight from London to Paris on May 16. Its partner 'Syrinx' made its first flight on May 17 and was awarded its C. of A. on June 8.

These newcomers carried 39 passengers with a crew of three, and although they never earned the affection bestowed on the Heracles and Hannibal types they gave reliable service until the start of World War II.

Their overall performance was comparable to that of the HP42 and with their wider capacity fuselages they offered a degree more of passenger comfort.

End of an Era

In general they remained on European service, with one exception when 'Syrinx' was chartered by Iraq Petroleum in connection with the opening of the Iraq-Mediterranean oil pipeline.

This was in January 1935 and is believed to be the only occasion when one of the Scyllas ventured far from its normal duties.

Later in the year 'Syrinx' suffered considerable damage when it was overturned by a violent gust while taxying at Brussels. Its rebuild was quite extensive and it was September 1936 before 'Syrinx' took to the air again.

The careers of these rather angular airliners ended in 1940; with 'Scylla' being wrecked in a gale in Scotland; and its partner 'Syrinx' ignominiously scrapped that same year.

Short L17 Scylla

Short L17 Syrinx

Short Empire Flying Boats S23 S30 S33

Without exception no other airliner of the 1930s had more influence on air travel than the graceful Empire flying boats. As a result of a British Government decision to carry all air mail without surcharge, their immediate priority was for a fleet of fast aircraft capable of fulfilling such a task.

Short Bros. was an obvious candidate, following their experience with the biplane Calcutta and Kent boats. Clearly these veterans were unequal to the challenge, and instead it led to the creation of a truly significant design; the Short S23; forerunner of the celebrated Empire boats.

The S23 emerged as a large four-engine monoplane of considerable beauty of line; with a payload of 3½ tons, inclusive of 1½ tons of mail and 24 day passengers or an alternative 16 sleeping-berth version.

Its design was remarkable for its time and in an unprecedented decision Imperial Airways ordered 28 examples straight off the drawing board. The prototype 'Canopus' took to the air on 4 July 1936 on its trouble-free maiden flight from Short Brother's works at Rochester.

On 31 October 'Canopus' inaugurated the Mediterranean service from Genoa; with the rest of the fleet following at an average of two per month.

From 4 February 1937, regular service on the Empire routes began at Hythe, with the last of the old overland services terminating at Croydon on 4 March. In conjunction with Qantas Empire Airways it was now possible to fly right through to Sydney in seven days, and in quite luxurious style.

By 1938 the Empire boats were operating services to Egypt, India, East Africa, Hong Kong and Australia; thereby superseding the older miscellaneous aircraft in service.

However there still remained the North Atlantic challenge; hitherto out of reach for commercial operation.

Consequently, one of the fleet, 'Caledonia' was fitted with long-range tanks and in December it carried out a series of non-stop survey flights of 12 hours endurance to the Mediterranean.

A proving flight over the North Atlantic to Canada was made on 5/6 July 1937, with 'Caledonia' eventually arriving in New York three days later. This flight left no margin for error; confirming that the S23s had not the endurance for a North Atlantic passenger crossing.

Three additional boats were delivered to Qantas in January 1938, bringing the S23 total to 31. These graceful boats were without exception the most famous and successful of all pre-war civil transports, but in their first two years of operations, their ranks were depleted in major fatal crashes.

Eight were lost in that period; with 'Capricornus' the shortest-lived of all the fleet; following a fatal crash in the Beaujolais Mountains on its maiden flight on 24 March 1937.

S30 and the Atlantic Air Mails

To enhance the S23's performance an improved version, the S30, powered by Bristol Perseus Radials in place of the original Bristol Pegasus was delivered in 1938-39.

Eight examples entered service, and in August 1939 'Cabot' and 'Caribou' inaugurated the North Atlantic mail route, just weeks before World War 2 intervened. Eight round trips were made; and a feature of these flights was the employment of Harrow tankers performing in-flight refuelling over Ireland.

Following the outbreak of war these boats were impressed into RAF service and operated with 119 Squadron on early A.S.V. radar trials. Unfortunately both were attacked and sunk by German aircraft during the abortive Norwegian campaign of May 1940.

Until December 1941 the Empire boats maintained a service through East Africa, India and Malaya to Australia, albeit in a less luxurious manner.

This link was irrevocably split by the Japanese occupation of Malaya in 1942, and in the desperate period of retreat through Sumatra and Java ten of these noble craft fell victim to Japanese attack.

Qantas 'Coolangatta' VH-ABB

A total of just thirteen S23, S30 and S33 boats were destined to survive the war and their useful lives were drawing to a close.

Too slow in comparison to a new generation of land planes and too expensive to maintain, in 1947 the veterans were broken up on Southampton Water. One of the first to go was the mighty 'Canopus', which had been in the vanguard of that fabulous era of international air travel only a decade earlier.

Over that period the Empire boats flew a grand total of 37,779,240 miles, over 2 million of which were flown by 'Canopus'.

Short Mayo Composite

The Empire boats had proven to be technologically ahead of any of their contemporaries; however one critical problem remained; lack of range.

This shortcoming was plainly evident in relation to the North Atlantic; despite a pressing need for long-distance mail and passenger flights to North America.

Admittedly a mail service was eventually inaugurated; but by then World War 2 was about to intervene and there was still the necessity for in-flight refuelling while the mail plane was in transit.

In 1935 the problem of lifting an overloaded mail plane into the air seemed insurmountable; nevertheless the Technical Manager at Imperial Airways came up with a bold solution. Robert Mayo's proposal was for a heavily loaded mail plane to be mounted on the back of a powerful but lightly loaded carrier aircraft.

At cruising altitude the two aircraft would separate; the carrier returning to base, while the mail plane, carrying more fuel than it could lift off the water under its own power, would proceed non-stop to its destination.

Despite the complexity of such a project, Imperial Airways received the go-ahead from Air Ministry and as a result an order was placed with Shorts to fulfil the order.

A modified Empire boat, fitted with a sturdy cradle to support the upper component was employed as the carrier plane; appropriately named 'Maia' (Mother).

The mail plane project involved the design and construction of a relatively large seaplane, capable of an Atlantic crossing with a full load of mail, newspapers, etc.

Short's response was the 'Mercury' (G-ADHJ) a well-proportioned twin-float design, powered by four 380hp Napier engines.

On 6 February 1938 the first in-flight separation tests were successfully carried out; and after further trials the Mayo Composite was delivered to Imperial Airways for experimental flights.

'Maia' G-ADHK

'Mercury's' pilot for these flights was Captain Donald Bennett; a 28 years old Australian, who after serving with the RAAF and RAF had joined Imperial Airways in 1936. Apart from being captain of the latest Empire flying boats at such a young age he was also a most competent navigator.

'Mercury' G-ADHJ

Atlantic Crossing

With such qualifications Bennett was entrusted with the first commercial flight across the Atlantic. Its two-man crew comprised Don Bennett and wireless operator J.D. Coster.

Space for 'Mercury's' crew was at a premium; however its cockpit was well arranged and with an efficient auto pilot.

On 20 July 1938 the Maia/Mercury composite took off and separated over Foynes in southern Ireland; with 'Mercury' carrying 600lbs of newspapers and newsreels.

New York and Return

A feature of North Atlantic weather conditions is a prevailing westerly wind pattern, and for 'Mercury's' crew this flight was no exception.

Bennett's navigational expertise was a key factor in this successful crossing to Montreal; a distance of 2,930 miles which was completed in 20hrs.20 mins. After refuelling they flew to New York, where their arrival was the subject of a frenzy of reporters and camera crews.

Their return flight was presented with some difficulties; as Mercury, even without payload could only lift less than one third of its maximum fuel load. This necessitated a fuel stop en-route at the Azores; from there to Lisbon and on to Southampton; thus completing the first transatlantic commercial flight.

World's Record Attempt

On arriving back in England Bennett approached the Air Ministry for their approval for an attempt on the World's long distance record for seaplanes; at that time held by Germany with a distance of 4,500 miles.

This proposal was accepted with enthusiasm and accordingly 'Mercury' underwent considerable modification at Short Bros. to increase the fuel capacity.

Dundee in Scotland was the departure point for the attempt; and on 6 October 1938 'Mercury' made a successful separation; with Cape Town the target for this strenuous two-day flight.

With such a fuel overload Bennett was obliged to use far wider throttle openings to maintain optimum air speed; and to compound the problem one of the engine cowlings had become loose and torn away, upsetting the streamlining of the nacelle.

For the first twelve hours the engines were continuously on full throttle, which speaks volumes for those hard-working Napiers. This factor was not their only problem; during a fuel transfer there was the stark realisation that the electric fuel pumps had ceased to function.

Fortunately there was an emergency manual pump for such a contingency; nevertheless it became an exhausting exercise to transfer fuel from the floats to the main wing tank.

Thanks to the auto pilot it was a task that could be shared between Bennett and his wireless operator Ian Harvey. As dawn approached on the second day it was clear that Cape Town was beyond their reach.

At least the World's seaplane record had been achieved, and the next priority was to find a suitable area in which to land Mercury.

Cape Town and Return

Alexander Bay at the mouth of the Orange River offered such an opportunity; and after a three hour refuelling operation they were on their way.

Cape Town was reached in mid-afternoon, thus completing a remarkable flight, with the seaplane record assessed at 6,000 miles non-stop in a time of 42½ hours.

Their return journey was a more leisurely affair, taking 6 days. This had been an important milestone in world aviation, yet neither Bennett nor his co-pilot received the slightest of plaudits from any source.

In 1940 'Mercury' was handed over to No320 Netherlands squadron where it was flown by Dutch pilots who managed to escape from Holland following the German invasion of the Low Countries.

Sadly this historic aircraft was returned to Shorts at Rochester in 1941 and there it was unceremoniously broken up. 'Maia', its partner from those ground-breaking flights was destroyed by enemy action at Poole, also in 1941.

DH Albatross

The creation of the DH91 Albatross can well be traced to the 1934 MacRobertson Air Race. The speed section of this prestigious event was won by the DH88 Comet, a purpose-built racing monoplane; but significantly in second place was the KLM DC2 airliner; while in third position was another airliner, the Boeing 247.

Understandably the performance of these new airliners, with their retractable undercarriage and all-metal construction had a profound effect on future British airliner designs.

Plainly the age of the biplane airliner had passed, and from that moment De Havilland worked tirelessly to have the Air Ministry accept the proposal that the firm should create a high speed airliner.

Eventually in January 1936 the Air Ministry placed an order for two examples of the DH 91 Albatross. De Havillands were already well advanced in the project and in May 1937 the prototype took to the air.

Surprisingly, in an emerging trend of all-metal types the Albatross was constructed in the traditional De Havilland style of spruce and laminated plywood; resulting nevertheless in one of the most beautiful transport aeroplanes ever built.

DH Albatross (Faraday)

A second prototype (G-AEVW) was also completed, and during a series of take-off tests the rear fuselage actually broke in two.

This setback could have been catastrophic but in a few weeks it re-appeared with the new and strengthened fuselage.

Albatross on European Service

Four Gypsy Twelve engines, faired in streamlined fashion into a graceful wing design provided a maximum speed of 220 mph with a range of 1040 miles.

Initially the type was intended for use as a North Atlantic mail carrier or transcontinental passenger liner; however they were destined to only operate on Imperial Airways European routes.

A total of seven of these elegant craft was built during 1937/38; and in their 'F' class 'Frobisher' category they settled down to fast, competitive schedules between Britain and the Continent, carrying 22 passengers and 4 crew.

Imperial also conducted experimental flights with the two long range mail plane versions, 'Faraday' and 'Franklin'; although they never proceeded further with the trials.

RAF Service

Their civil careers were abruptly terminated with the outbreak of World War 2, but they continued to serve as transports with RAF units; with wartime camouflage applied over their once-pristine silver surfaces.

Sad to relate, not one example survived the hostilities; with 'Faraday' and 'Franklin' destroyed in crashes at Reykjavik in 1941; and 'Fingal' and 'Fortuna' suffering a similar fate in the United Kingdom.

'Frobisher' became a victim of German bombs during the 1940 Blitz; and with spares almost non-existent, 'Fiona' and 'Falcon' were broken up in September 1943.

Armstrong Whitworth Ensign

Armstrong Whitworth were responsible for the construction of three significant types operated by Imperial Airways; beginning with the angular tri-motor Argosy biplane of 1926 vintage.

This was followed in 1932 by the AW15 Atalanta; a high-wing monoplane of exceptionally clean aerodynamic form.

Their AW27 Ensign was by far the largest pre-war landplane design to enter Imperial service; and like the Atalanta it was a four-motor high wing monoplane, but there any similarity ended.

This newcomer was almost twice the physical size, three times the all-up weight, of all-metal construction and fitted with an enormous retractable undercarriage. Its design was inspired by a 1934 Government decision to carry all first-class Empire mail by air.

As a consequence an order was placed in 1935 for 12 machines; later increased to 14 to fulfil the task.

At the time Armstrong Whitworth were working to capacity on the new Whitley bomber; as a result all airliner construction took place at another venue.

This extended the building and test flight programme until 24 January 1938 when the prototype 'Ensign' (G-ADSR) first took to the air. Apart from an unscheduled forced landing during flight trials due to fuel starvation, 'Ensign' qualified for its Certificate of Airworthiness and flew its first service to Paris on 20 October 1938.

Twenty seven passengers were carried on these flights; with later versions accommodating forty on the European routes.

Shortly afterwards three Ensigns were used to fly the 1938 Christmas mail to Australia, but all three fell by the wayside with engine problems, which saw them returned to the makers.

The original Tiger IX motors proved unequal to the task; and as a result they were fitted with the more powerful Tiger IXc version. However these delays prevented any further Ensign involvement on Empire routes.

With the outbreak of war in 1939 the Ensigns were impressed into RAF service; and in the hectic 1939/40 period three were lost to enemy action.

In order to improve their performance the remainder were re-engined with 950hp Wright Cyclones, and in that format they continued to give sterling service to Africa and the Near East.

The last Ensign civil passenger flight was on 3 June 1946; following that, each of the once-proud Ensigns made its last flight to its birthplace, Hamble and then to be unceremoniously broken up.

AW Ensign G-ADSR

Short 'G' Class boats

The S26 'G' class boats represented the company's final pre-war flying boat design. Three examples were built for Imperial Airways; beginning with 'Golden Hind' (G-AFCI) which was launched in June 1939.

The second and third were completed as 'Golden Fleece' (G-AFCJ) and 'Golden Horn' (G-AFCK). Although they superficially resembled the S23 and S30 Empire boats the S26 was considerably larger.

Powered by four 1,380hp Bristol Hercules they gave a cruising range of 3,000 miles with normal fuel loadings.

From the outset they were designed for the North Atlantic route, but with the outbreak of war, any transatlantic aspirations came to an end.

Instead they were initially commandeered into RAF service with 119 Coastal Command Squadron for long range reconnaissance duties. Their conversion entailed the fitting of rear and dorsal turrets, internal depth charge housing, plus a full camouflage scheme.

BOAC Ownership

'Golden Fleece' was lost in August 1941, after the failure of two engines off Finisterre; with the surviving crew members being picked up by an enemy submarine.

Following the disbandment of 119 squadron, 'Golden Hind' and 'Golden Horn' were converted to civil operation under BOAC ownership. Operating from Poole they maintained a vital service between the United Kingdom and West Africa via Lisbon.

Forty passengers and diplomatic mail were carried; however these seats were restricted to high priority persons.

The careers of these graceful craft were to end in ignominious fashion; with 'Golden Horn' crashing into Lisbon's River Tagus in January 1943 with the loss of 13 occupants. 'Golden Hind' survived the war and passed through various operators until 1954 when it was sunk while under tow from Hamble.

Short 'Golden Hind' G-AFCI

'Golden Horn' in wartime BOAC livery after wing-tip float repairs at Lisbon January 1943. That same month it was involved in a crash on the river Tagus with 13 deaths, including the pilot, Captain J.H. Lock.

Imperial Airways and British Airways Amalgamation

In June 1939 Parliament introduced a bill aimed at forming British Overseas Airways by amalgamating Imperial Airways with British Airways. This passed its second reading in the House of Commons with a majority of 79.

On 4 August Royal Assent was given to the bill and the merger took place on 1 April 1940, seven months after the start of World War II.

Perhaps there was something prophetic about the date; for it was on 1April 1924 that Imperial Airways was officially launched; having had been created as part of government policy to run the overseas routes of the Empire.

From the outset it was a public limited company formed from five small companies, and proved to be a most successful operation, both technically and operationally. Imperial did receive a small subsidy from the Empire mail scheme, but otherwise had practically no government aid.

During that pioneering era, notably the 1920s it forged routes over areas that were hostile in the extreme for aviation.

Notwithstanding the limited technology available, Imperial Airways fleet of landplanes and seaplanes gave the intrepid air traveller an opportunity to traverse the globe to destinations hitherto out of reach. Such progress was occasionally dogged by tragedy, which was an inevitable consequence of early air travel.

However when one considers the vast distances covered by those veteran airliners, in conditions that were often treacherous their safety record was remarkable.

Another factor for British prestige was the fact that throughout its tenure Imperial Airways ongoing range of aircraft were of British design and construction. There were several possible exceptions, one being the Avro Ten tri-motor of 1930 vintage, which was essentially an Anglicized version of the successful Fokker FVII series.

During the 1930s the biplane airliner had largely been supplanted by an emerging range of four-engine types; typified by the successful S23 and S30 Empire boats. Two landplane types also deserve mention; De Havilland's graceful Albatross and the impressive Armstrong Whitworth Ensign.

Conversely, Imperial's rival during the late 1930s, British Airways operated mostly with foreign aircraft; Dutch, German and American; without ever operating British aircraft on a regular basis.

Significantly Imperial Airways consistently paid a small dividend to its shareholders; while British Airways was never financially successful.

Whatever the government's motivation in dismantling Imperial, it could be regarded as political vindictiveness. Imperial Airways always supported the British aircraft industry; a situation that would end under the new regime.

In a final statement an ungrateful Conservative government refused to recommend any honours for those pioneers who had done so much British and world aviation.

Admittedly the managing director George Woods Humphreys was given a grant by the company but otherwise he received nothing. Neither he nor Colonel Burchell, the General Manager Administration nor Major Bob Mayo, the General Manager Technical received any honours for the pioneering work they had done.

Imperial Airways at that time was the major airline of the world; while its machines were almost entirely the four-engine aircraft which it had itself pioneered; covering half the world with its routes.

In summary its amalgamation with British Airways needs to be regarded as a retrograde action, while the government's treatment of those Imperial pioneers was quite deplorable.

Flying Matilda

Pioneers of Australian Aviation

Murray McLeod

Flying Matilda presents a selection of historic events in early Australian aviation. The iconic Kingsford Smith, Bert Hinkler and other greats feature in this illustrated volume by Australian artist and author Murray McLeod. Born in Sydney, Murray is a published illustrator and writer with his motorcycle and aviation books and magazines.

Flying Matilda
Pioneers of early Australian aviation

On August 4 1914, following Germany's violation of Belgian neutrality, Great Britain who had pledged to support that country declared war on Germany. The Australian Government was quick to offer military aid to the Mother Country and recruiting began on 8 August, with the expectation of raising a force of at least 20,000 men. That target was easily reached; which saw the formation of the First Australian Division; such was the fervour of Australians to go to Britain's assistance. Five infantry divisions and one Light Horse division were eventually raised as the A.I.F. (Australian Imperial Force), which over the ensuing four years of war went on to provide 460,000 able-bodied men for overseas service.

A significant feature of the AIF was that every member was a volunteer. On two occasions, when enlistments fell short, Prime Minister Hughes called a referendum to introduce conscription; and in both instances it was defeated. During its four-year period of active service the AIF gained a fighting reputation that was unsurpassed. But with such an involvement came a battle casualty rate of 64%; higher than any army of the British Empire. Sixty thousand AIF troops were killed or died of wounds, while 152,000 were wounded, which for a population of just 4.8 million these were saddening statistics. Barely a family was spared to mourn the loss or incapacitation of a loved one.

At the outbreak of war the aeroplane had barely advanced beyond the designs created by the Wright brothers in 1903; while very few Australians had been near or actually seen an aeroplane. All that changed dramatically after the ill-starred Gallipoli campaign of 1915; when following the AIF's return to Egypt in December, and its enlargement to four divisions, the embryonic Australian Flying Corps was created. Four squadrons were raised; with No.1 remaining in the Middle East, and Nos.2, 3 and 4 proceeding to the Western Front. From mid-1917 until the Armistice of November 1918 they made a great contribution to victory for the Allied powers. Airmen from all parts of the British Empire also served in great numbers with Royal Flying Corps squadrons, but throughout that period the Australian Flying Corps was the only Dominion force that operated as an independent air arm.

Far reaching consequences were a feature of the Great War; with significant changes occurring in Europe, where new frontiers and states were created. Many of the Royal Houses disappeared; never to return; and what had been achieved?

A generation of young men had been swept away; but a country's ruined economy does not reflect its greatest cost; this can be restored by the right men. It is the loss of the right men, the flower of a nation which represents its greatest loss.

The science that created weapons with which to conduct the war had surged ahead in an almost obscene manner. It became possible to destroy your fellow man in swift, impersonal fashion with a bewildering array of high explosive, machine guns and poison gas.

By far the greatest advances in technology were in the air; starting with the antiquated types of 1914. From those faltering beginnings they progressed in steady fashion to iconic fighter aircraft such as the Sopwith Snipe and Fokker D7.

The Snipe represented the final lineage in a series of rotary engine scouts built by Sopwith, and went on to serve in the post war RAF for a number of years. Fokker's classic D7 with its efficient BMW engine could be regarded as the greatest fighter of the war.

It was significant that one of the conditions of the Armistice was that all the D7s were to be handed over to the Allies. Also noteworthy was the new generation of large aircraft. Two prime examples were the Vickers Vimy and Handley Page 0/400; heavy bomber designs that were readily converted to airliners in the post war period.

Following the Armistice there was a host of young Australian airmen virtually out of a job and impatient to be on their way home. Intense interest was aroused in 1919 when the Australian Government offered a prize of £10,000 for the first Australian crew to make a flight from England to Australia in less than 30 days.

Two brothers, Ross and Keith Smith achieved that goal in just over 28 days. Theirs was a remarkable effort, considering the primitive ground facilities of the time and in an aircraft that was basic in instrumentation and performance.

Australia in the 1920s was an embryo period in civil aviation; where in the main the pilots had wartime experience, which they applied to a civil career. All too often their attitude was a cavalier approach to their profession, appropriate to the Western Front but hardly acceptable to a nervous passenger making his first flight.

Two notable exceptions were Lt. Hudson Fysh, who went on to create the international airline Qantas; and Major Norman Brearley who began a modest air taxi service which emerged as West Australian Airlines.

Australia was blessed with a host of local heroes and without doubt the 'supremo' was Charles Kingsford Smith. His list of record-breaking flights was most impressive; with his 1928 Pacific Crossing arguably at the top of the list.

Other pioneers also deserve mention; Bert Hinkler, the light-plane specialist and a superb navigator. P.G. Taylor is remembered for his survey flights across the South Pacific and for his award of the George Cross in 1935 for a feat of incredible bravery.

During the early 1930s Australia had its share of airline tragedies, as pilots battled the elements in machines that carried the most basic of safety aids. By then the swashbuckling flier had been relegated to history.

In his place came a generation of analytical and prudent pilots who steered Australian aviation towards the respected reputation it enjoys to this day.

These following articles give a brief insight to the fortunes of those pioneering Australian airmen.

Some survived their experiences and had the satisfaction of witnessing the results of those hard-won lessons.

But all too often they became victims of the law of averages when they set out on that final flight.

For Valour
The air VCs of World War II

Murray McLeod

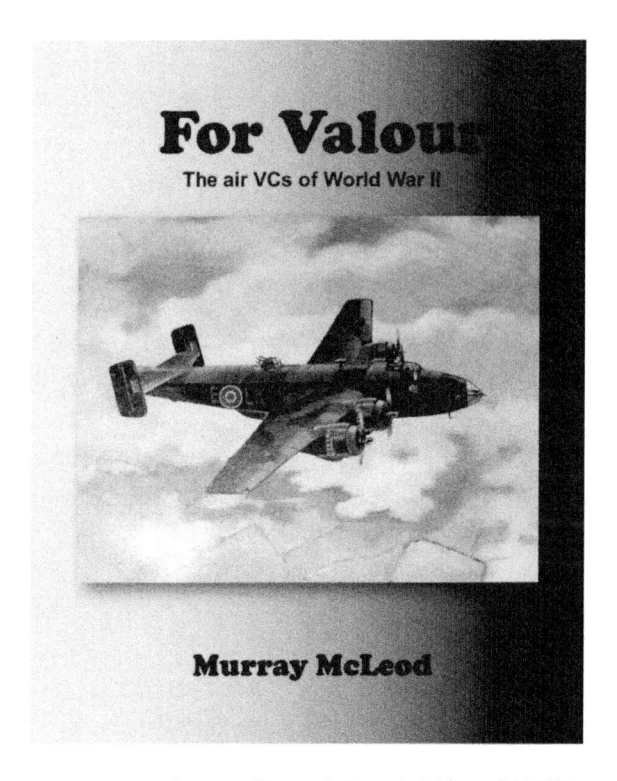

For Valour contains profiles of the air VCs of WWII and their aircraft. Airmen from Bomber, Fighter and Coastal Command are featured in this illustrated volume by accomplished Australian artist and author Murray McLeod. The aircraft types involved in the conflict are also profiled making this book a tribute to an elite group of airmen, and their particular aircraft.

They answered the call to arms with quiet determination, to give of their best whatever the challenge and however great the odds.

For Valour
Air VCs of World WAR II

For Valour is arranged in alphabetical rather than chronological order and it is fitting that the Avro Lancaster heads the list. No less than ten V.C.s were awarded to Lancaster crew, which made a selection of the most spectacular of those incidents a challenging task. The writer elected to portray the daylight Augsburg raid of 17 April 1942 and the subsequent award of the Victoria Cross to Sqdrn. Ldr. J.D. Nettleton, the first of ten gained by Lancaster crewmembers. Whether he was the pilot or another crewmember, each of the 32 VC recipients displayed that selfless devotion in the fulfilment of his mission, and in every case against odds that seemed insurmountable.

The Victoria Cross represents Britain's highest award for bravery in the face of the enemy. The actual medal consists of a bronze Maltese cross suspended from a burgundy ribbon, and on the medal is cast a modest inscription; 'For Valour.' During World War 2 a total of 32 V.C.s were awarded to aircrew from the United Kingdom and the Dominions.

By far the majority went to Bomber Command, which is understandable when one considers the magnitude of its operations. Occupied Europe was the main arena in a relentless campaign instigated by the War Council and prosecuted by Air Chief Marshall Harris during his tenure as Bomber Command 'supremo'.

At the end of hostilities in Europe, and when the costs were assessed, Bomber Command alone had suffered a loss rate of 47,000 aircrew. It was a sobering statistic and highlighted the fact that airmen were confronted with odds far more daunting than those faced by a front line soldier in World War 1.

In such an environment it was inevitable that instances of extreme gallantry would emerge. In the case of heavy bombers any recipient of the ultimate award had the advantage of crewmembers to verify the deed.

All too often these awards were posthumous; so extreme were the circumstances that generally faced aircrew. Some recipients returned to operations following their award, and in three instances these airmen paid the ultimate sacrifice. Thus, at the close of hostilities, only eight VC winners had survived the conflict.

For five long years Coastal Command waged a relentless war against the U-boat and enemy shipping.

For some aircrew it became a series of extended patrols over hostile waters without the opportunity of action.

While for others it was the complete reverse, with running battles in their ponderous flying boats against roving long-range fighters. Coastal Command's priority was the destruction of the predatory U-boat, whose sinking of merchant ships brought England to the point of strangulation.

Attacking a surfaced U-boat became an extremely hazardous operation when it elected to challenge an attacking aircraft.

It took considerable nerve on the part of the pilot to run the gauntlet of concentrated fire from the U-boat during the unwavering run-in to the target. On three occasions a Victoria Cross was awarded to pilots as a result of their personal dedication and with the support of crew members in such situations.

The Fleet Air Arm produced two V.C. winners, both posthumous, and in aircraft of vastly different performance and vintage.

Their machines are worthy of comparison; one being a venerable Fairey Swordfish biplane with its open cockpits and 100 mph maximum speed, and the other a state-of-the-art carrier fighter, the versatile Vought F4U Corsair.

Single-seat aircraft featured on only two occasions; the first was to a Hurricane pilot in August 1940 during the Battle of Britain and the second was the Corsair pilot in August 1945.

Transport Command was an unlikely category but it did occur during the ill-starred Arnhem assault in September 1944. The pilot of the Dakota involved was on a heroic supply mission and again the award was posthumous.

The following pages feature the19 types of aircraft involved in the gaining of that supreme award, plus an account of the events that led to it.

Readers might express surprise at the absence of famous types, such as the Spitfire, Mosquito, Sunderland and others, despite their involvement in the conflict.

Nevertheless, they need to be remembered alongside the types that were involved in the awards. The supreme gallantry displayed by aircrew was never in question, but did their equipment match that sacrifice? Front-line types, such as the Bristol Blenheim and Fairey Battle that entered RAF service prior to the outbreak of war were found to be quite inadequate in the harsh realities of combat. The Fairey Swordfish biplane was an anachronism with its lack of speed and armament, and yet it remained operational throughout the conflict; its success due mainly to the dedication of its crews.

The RAF's greatest disappointment was surely the Avro Manchester, due to the total unreliability of its undeveloped Vulture engines, but from that disaster came the mighty Lancaster, Bomber Command's finest aircraft. Some types, such as the Hampden and Stirling were found to be a disappointment in fulfilling their designer's sanguine expectations. Again it was their crews who created any reputation that was accorded the actual aircraft. American designs are featured in six of the following accounts, and with one possible exception; the Lockheed Ventura, they were machines worthy of the crews who took the fight to the enemy.

ELLIOTT'S ODYSSEY

MURRAY McLEOD

Soldier of fortune, James Elliott's quest for adventure takes him to the skies of the Western Front and Middle East. In a post-war situation he becomes involved in a sobering campaign in North Russia against the Bolsheviks, and later a successful Atlantic crossing by airship.

The culmination of his restless wanderings is achieved in a pilgrimage to the old battlefields of Gallipoli as a member of a group of ex-servicemen.

Growing up in suburban Sydney, Doug Stewart endures a strained relationship with his father who is embittered by his Western Front experiences. As an air gunner in a later conflict Doug suffers trauma as an airmen during his service with Bomber Command. For the first time in his life he has no choice but to face the same forces that crafted his father's difficulties. In a post-war world he must conquer those personal demons to re-attach the missing links from his own wartime experiences and to unearth those answers to his father's pilgrimage.

Murray McLeod does not disappoint in his second novel where he draws a stark and moving account of men in armed conflict. The novel brings a compelling read that covers two generations of fighting men - their struggles and their family lives. *The Pilgrimage* follows on from Murray's success with his debut novel *Elliot's Odyssey*.

Printed in Great Britain
by Amazon